DISTANT EARLY WARNING

DISTANT EARLY WARNING

POEMS BY RAD SMITH

FOREWORD BY DONALD HALL

COVER PHOTOGRAPH:
Twenty Sticks, Kohoku, Honshu, Japan. 2003 © Michael Kenna

AUTHOR PHOTOGRAPH: Jim Rippe

LIBRARY OF CONGRESS CONTROL NUMBER: 2004115647

ISBN: 0–9762947–0–2

THE MIRA PRESS
P.O. Box 590207
Newton Centre, MA 02459

themirapress@rcn.com

for Rena

ACKNOWLEDGMENTS

Grateful acknowledgment is made to the editors of the following magazines in which poems appeared, some in earlier versions and some with different titles:

Antigonish Review: "Daphne," "Heavy Water," "Leaf Boat," "Meteorites," "Old Fisherman," "Your Caller";

The Chacalaca Review: "Crack Shot," "Morning With Pine Pollen";

The Hiram Poetry Review: "A Long Hot Sentence For You";

Lyric (City Lights): "Mud Season," "To A Nightingale";

The MacGuffin: "Grandfather Loses His Mind";

Poetry: "Writing In Water," "Requiem Shark," "Help," "Say Water," "Before It's Too Late";

Poetry Northwest: "Fathers of Daughters";

Poetry Motel: "Bread";

Prairie Schooner: "Blanca And Miranda," "DEW Line," "Mixed Vegetables," "Only Fireflies," "To The Next Reader Of The Book I Take To Bed With Me," "The Man Who Cannot Stop Crying";

The Spoon River Anthology: "Frankenstein's Monster";

Wild Earth: "Abundance."

*   *   *   *

Although Rad dedicated this book to me, without the encouragement of Barbara and Wendy, it would have remained an unpublished manuscript. Rad's sister, Emily Smith, is owed special thanks. Of course our children, Zandy and Jordan, are at the core of everything I do and I thank them more than they can ever know.

RK

CONTENTS

TWO

Though not one to put much stock in things meant
to be, I am almost tempted to alter my point of view.
Or perhaps, it is just another example of suddenly
noticing today something that has always been around—
something whose name you only learned yesterday. At
any rate, I have recently begun to feel the need to
decompress, to emerge from my self-imposed isolation
to gulp with others the invigorating oxygen of poetry.
I think these poems should give you some idea of
what I do . . .

RAD SMITH
9/8/96

ABOUT THE AUTHOR

If Rad had lived to write this, it would have been brief. He would
have said that he loved wild places and clear lakes, and that his great-
est accomplishments were a loving marriage of almost twenty years
and being the father of two extraordinary children.

Rad was born in 1947 in Iowa City, Iowa. He grew up in St. Cloud,
Minnesota, and attended Harvard College, where he studied with
Elizabeth Bishop. He was an athlete: an All-American swimmer and a
nidan in uechi-ryu karate, who founded a dojo in Charlottesville,
Virginia, which spun off schools in Georgia and in Germany. For
more than twenty-five years he studied Japanese swords as art objects,
and the depth of his knowledge in this field earned him a national
reputation.

After two years of teaching in Harlem, Rad attended The Harvard
Business School and worked as an executive in a high-technology
firm for fifteen years. But he was dissatisfied. Finally, with much
trepidation, he decided to make a major life change.

Thus he began the last phase of his life: car-pooling, grocery
shopping, building a house in Maine and a tree house in Newton,
and writing poetry. Poetry had been his love even as a young boy
and throughout college, but he did not write a word during the
fifteen years he spent in the business world. Now poems exploded
out of him. After writing in solitude for several years, he entered The
Workshop for Publishing Poets in Brookline, Massachusetts. It was
there, with the critical ear and eye of Barbara Helfgott Hyett and the
support and stimulation of other poets, that his writing sharpened and
blossomed.

In June 1998, we were stunned to learn that he was in the final
stage of lung cancer. A bitter irony for a man who had never smoked
a cigarette. In spite of the devastating news, he signed up for the
fall poetry class, and racing against the growing tumors, began to
assemble this manuscript. The support from his poet friends was
exceptional. A group gathered from the workshop: Barbara and Eric
Hyett, Wendy Mnookin, Art Nayhill, Adnan Onart, Alan West and

Martha Wright. They met with Rad to read and discuss his poems. In a letter about these sessions he wrote," . . . you work all week on a 50 line poem you think is good, and you find only 6 worthwhile lines in it." On Halloween, Rad entered the hospital for the last time. While he still had some strength, Barbara and Wendy would visit. Ignoring the tubes and the distractions, they talked, read to him and continued their endless discussion of poetry.

Rad died the morning of December 7, 1998, during the few minutes in weeks that he was not surrounded by his family. Three days before, he convinced one of the nurses to wheel his bed into the hospital courtyard. Outside for the final time, the unusually warm air rustling his bed sheets, Rad turned and whispered, "Life is definitely worth living."

RENA KOOPMAN

NEWTON, MASSACHUSETTS
MAY 2004

FOREWORD

In a note, Rad Smith speaks of feeling "the need . . . to gulp with others the invigorating oxygen of poetry." *Distant Early Warning* reminds me of why I love this art so much. Of the natural world he makes such memorable images, phrases of physical detail that fix a moment and leave it hovering in the mind. Of seagulls he notes "the intravenous drip / of their voices, their unsteady wings." "Mixed Vegetables" wonderfully preserves passion for the body of the world. "I dream of tomatoes," he writes, and "Days I walk through narrow streets / cobbled with onions." When he meditates "on my deck of empty seed packets" he tells us that he listens "for the first sign of trouble — / a seed coat splitting, a tiny click / like when a lock's tumbler slips." The lover remains alert for danger.

"Morning with Pine Pollen" describes the natural scene with a fine attention, and then observes another presence. "I find it difficult to watch you / vanish through a wall of sunlight . . . " The poem ends with the woman — it has to be a woman — "smiling / even as you glance back / and wave at me / through the glittering that stabs skyward." It is a happy scene; menace survives in "stabs." His book's title alerts us to the menace that his poems are full of. But his sense of threat walks always in the company of joy. In "Abundance"—a quality branded on Smith's sensibility—he praises "the generosity of purple plums." In a storm, "the roof shudders like horses." The poems are not only visually acute but witty. He "cannot bear / to watch the sky change / out of its navy blue / into something more comfortable . . . "

Smith's poems are crowded with people, especially of the female persuasion—loves, old lovers, daughters. ("Fathers of Daughters" is a favorite of mine.) Many of the poems I love best are too long to quote in full. Here's a short one, love among the ruins.

BEES

Look! Our storm-thrashed garden,
that parade of ants tottering
about on high heels waving rose

petal parasols: the same petals
in which yesterday I watched bees,
one after another—bandy legs
glittering with gold—
enjoy themselves, and which
tomorrow at breakfast
will blossom on your lips.

Blossom is beauty and sting. In "Meteorites" Smith ends with "that
blue sky / fully armed and dangerous." This is a poetry of affection, of
joy in the world—and of appropriate dread.

When I first read the poems of Rad Smith, I wrote his widow: "As
you might imagine, I have seen many manuscripts by people whom I
have not known, and over the last fifty years I have read thousands
and thousands of poems in manuscript. There is only one other occa-
sion when I read a collection with so much enthusiasm."

We have lost a precious maker, losing Rad Smith.

DONALD HALL

One

SAY WATER

Say *birds* instead of *water*
because birds are signing
to each other
in the fluttery
language of water.

Or say *deer* and lift your head
as if you sense my mouth
drinking from your glass
because deer have trampled the water
and left it nervous.

Or pines, say *pines*,
their needles brushing
across my body must by now
know something of trembling.

No, say *water* in that limpid voice
you once used to draw the icy bath
when I, wild-tongued, was burning up
and you were beautiful.

Cancer?

talk of the fragile

BEES

Look! Our storm-thrashed garden,
that parade of ants tottering
about on high heels waving rose
petal parasols: the same petals
in which yesterday I watched bees,
one after another—bandy legs
glittering with gold—
enjoy themselves, and which
tomorrow at breakfast
will blossom on your lips.

ZEN GARDEN

The sand must be picked clean
then raked into oceans and fields
mounds of azaleas clipped
into a single point of view
every third pine needle plucked
and the distant mountain
borrowed back from the mist
before I can bear to watch you
scatter over the swept path
over the moss
brushed soft as a hound's ear
those few fiery maple leaves
that will burn for days.

one sentence

THE MOON IN THE RIVER

—or rather the memory of the river
bearing the moon below the orchard
where we picked tart green dusty apples
and lay out all night on a blanket,
naked it was so warm.

I want too much of everything,
especially
what is deserting me—
silence
howling through silence.

I want the rider without his horse,
the implication
not the statement.
The beating
not the heart.

the life

I'll bring you the cores in a wicker basket
lined with a linen napkin. Don't forget
the seeds. *Yes.* The seeds.

consider everything

MIXED VEGETABLES

All night I dream of tomatoes,
sun-simmering vats of them.
Days I walk through narrow streets
cobbled with onions.
When I make love the kiss
just afterward tastes of arugula.
And when I move along the rows
tapping out seeds from the torn
corner of each packet, sprinkling them
like candies on a cake, I move
with a slow vegetable grace.

Such command
every line a poem

But everything goes wrong.
In the same moist furrow,
carrots fall in with burdock,
spinach with rutabaga.
I worry about the broccoli: a dainty
floret knocked up by a cabbage,
or strangled by a string bean.
And what about summer squash and snow peas?
A mess like my daughter's belief
an Episcopalian Messiah will save one half
of her, but which half?, she asks,
my son who wants to wear
a yarmulke to church.

I sit cross-legged, meditating
on my deck of empty seed packets.
I listen for the first sign of trouble—
a seed coat splitting, a tiny click
like when a lock's tumbler slips.

SCIENTISTS NOW BELIEVE

—for Jack Thayer

blue jays reforested North America
after the last ice age.
Another creature to feel grateful for
as I lie in bed
listening to the bitter
shrieking in the Japanese maple,
its dry leaves,
the crackling in my lung,
with the folded white silk offering scarf,
which the Dalai Lama gave to my friend Jack
when they knocked foreheads,
resting on my forehead.
Knocked was Jack's word,
not touched or pressed
which is what my forehead feels
of the silk right now.
Not that thwack to the skull, the blow
aimed at the live
center of the whole churning universe,
the acorn cracked, broken,
or scattered. All of us.

WHAT I WANTED TO TAKE HOME
FROM GREECE

Not the Parthenon. Too much
remains. But that handful of meanders
I excavated in the shadow of one
of its perfect columns
when nobody was looking,

like the seeds
the beat
not the heart

fragments needing
a lip to pour from, a throat
to restrain, a belly to hold
what the foot must support.

I was beginning to write
then, struggling,
but it wasn't just that.

Did I really think
I could get away with it:
compose a whole urn
out of losses, fool
the guards at the border?

EVEN ONE

Unbuckle my money belt,
watch, my halter of keys.
Saw off this insatiable
ring that chokes me.

Isn't one armless torso enough?
If we had a thousand paintings by Leonardo
instead of twelve,
would I love him less?

How many trunkfuls of treasure
lie unclaimed? And what of my house
garrisoned with knickknacks,
my masks, my deft delinquencies?

Look at the trees chattering.
Each ice-thorned branch tempts
the wind with its fragility.
Of my five hundred poems, who knows
even one.

One is important

ONLY FIREFLIES   *taken two ways*

exploding against the windshield
like tiny Molotov cocktails.
And frogs. For miles they bounce
across the road, the wheels
crushing them until I grow used
to a certain bumpiness in the ride.

← only one good contrast

Now a buck raises his head,
a glowing cigarette eye.
What if he should leap
headlong into my lights and be struck?
Would he twitch quietly beside the car
while I, injured myself, cried over him?

Or stagger to his feet and charge
into the woods, struggling
toward a music he had to get closer to?
Would it be the song I hear
sometimes late at night on the radio,

that singer who wanders from one
station to another? No encore
this evening, she hopes, because
despite the applause, she's tired,
and her voice is giving out.

Death is tired?

DEW LINE

This morning I watch an eagle bearing north
toward spiked antennas of the *DEW* line,
and feel a sadness I cannot get enough of,
or is it the emptiness beyond
this consumptive little harbor—

a wildness I want as I want to believe
that sighting of a mountain lion near Katahdin,
its soft whistle call and a cry
like a woman in pain. But I hear
only my neighbor talking to herself.

We squint awkwardly at each other
across our crumbling chunk of Atlantic coastline
before she slips out of her bathrobe,
nightgown, slippers, watch, and dives
into the cold kelpy swells because

the door creaks, the phone rings
or doesn't, the flowers offend her,
because the gulls are wobbling
overhead, the intravenous drip
of their voices, their unsteady wings.

THE CLIFFS
—at Cape St. Mary's

If the fall doesn't kill you
instantly, the icy water will,
unless by some miracle—
those cliffs waste no time plunging
into the broken ribcage of the North Atlantic—
you're seized, lifted,
thrust into the deranged migration
of pitch-tipped wings.
Such arid irises. Don't you
recognize yourself?

Don't call it sacrifice, or submission.
Certainly not salvation. Think of it
as terms of employment, ethereal
and theatrical in a grand opera staged by Blake
with angel-birds, and you
as the sole human chosen
to spin endlessly clockwise.

MAGNUS ANNUS
—after Yeats

That tiger that once vanished
to such applause paces here,
still invisible, still snarling.
I hear him now at my wrist,
that steady pace of his,
advancing. I have taken

too much for granted.
Others leave tracks— | *dying*
I have been writing for days,
this poem, these words,
so they will flash
through earth, fire, water, air,
and whatever else is there.

Tonight, I cannot bear
to watch the sky change
out of its navy blue
into something more comfortable,
or hail the comet,
its icy smudge. Aries
is inching eastward.
The Goat has strayed.

ABUNDANCE

1.

Doesn't the sun show favor to my field—
potatoes large as melons, sultry kale,
the generosity of purple plums.
I dip my hands into the hive. At night the sky
out of its great confectionery basin
shakes a dust of stars. Grayling and bream
leap onto the bank to kiss my feet.

2.

I'm afraid of leaves and listening
to the gentle rain. I shudder
at its emotion, the oblivion
of the river that coils around my house.
The great triple-trunked oak struck
by lightning rots into mushrooms beneath
a thatch of cornflowers. The mice increase.
Woodpeckers are tearing the world apart.

LEAF BOAT

Tiny bugs on this maple leaf
are jumping, scads of them.
A hyperactive halftime marching band.
Oh, the pile-ups, the strange
(don't they get it?) conjunctions.

Now they surge starboard,
a magnet pulling them,
or has the captain just announced
a once-in-a-lifetime sight-
seeing opportunity off the bow
that none of them want to miss.

But wait. They're running back.
Somebody must have noticed the flames
breaking out along leaflines
and pulled the alarm.

They're all stamping
like mad on the sparks,
the sodium-orange veins.

It's only going to get
madder and madder.
And then they're going down.

inevitability

smallness
helplessness

TRESPASS

The boy unbuttons his shirt,
steps out of his jeans, snakes
coiling around the muscular barge
of his chest, forked tongues, fangs.

Out of the whirlwind at his navel
lightning strikes his heart.
A green lizard crawls
into the crack of his ass.

The girl is blooming with calla lilies.
Goldfish tangle in the pool of her belly,
quiver when she laughs.
Big red lips suck on her breasts,

and vines of honeysuckle, half-finished,
climb each leg as if
the tattoos are growing-in
naturally like body hair.

She wades in up to her crotch,
splashes her underarms, rubs her face.
Then, he charges in kicking,
gasping, thrashing.

Soon they're floating together in the thin
layer of warm water, cold burning
inches beneath them, just their noses
and her nipples bobbing like tiny buoys.

ANOTHER LITTLE EXERCISE
—after Elizabeth Bishop

Think of mosquitoes probing the screen,
testing each mesh desperate for a way in.

Think what the water, twitching and darkening
really wants from the mountain

because maybe it's not
extending a gracious invitation.

Think of the man across the lake hammering.
Every few minutes he yells, then curses

the broken board, the nail, his hammer.
He's been working since dawn.

Think of me sitting quietly
on the screened porch. Think of me
listening and writing everything down.

OLD FISHERMAN

A fisherman below the dam casts time
and time again into the fast water
without catching anything. Failure
seems to focus him, or the laughter
of women on the bank.

I watch him try to hook the sky
to water, his rod twitching.
The stretched line nurses in the foam.

I want to ask him why he doesn't
cast upstream into the jade
green water where fish
loll in the current among the horsetails.

But then, he is on the opposite shore,
and I am still young enough
to waste another forty years
complicating my life.

The fisherman is simple.
It is about the casting, not the fish caught

BEFORE IT'S TOO LATE

Build the perfect house, then burn it down:
every vaulted ceiling, the vitrine
of skeleton clocks, the stained
glass window. You can do better.

If while tipping the can of gasoline
or striking the match, you hesitate,
think of Euripides in his cave,
those characters in seventy-one lost plays.

How afterward, there will still be enough
to worry about, and nothing worth saving.
Think of the expense. Just the taxes.
All those shutters to paint.

Besides, eventually the roof will leak.   ) Inevitability
Somebody will break in, vandalize the place,
take everything valuable, not appreciate
any of it. Not be frightened by it.

MUD SEASON

Our road a trough of mud, the spring
sinkhole where I stand helplessly throwing
sticks under the tires of the electric
company truck while the driver rocks
gently back and forth. Suddenly
he pounds the horn, the steering wheel and
floors it. The tires whine, his curses wail
across the lake, across class lines,
across his boss's back until
the windows shake the trees reflected in them,
and the miles on the dashboard
advance so fast he could be halfway
to the moon. Except he starts
laughing. Then I laugh. Soon
the truck's laughing
even as the wheel rims churn deep
and deeper.

MISCUTS

Sawdust settles over my tools
in drifts of cinnamon and gold,
over my last sharp pencil,
calculations for bookshelves,
phone numbers, notes for poems
I will never write scrawled
on end-checked scraps of wood.

If you could see me ankle-deep
in cypress and cocobolo
shavings, persimmon chips, splinters
of satinwood, kindling I shall
blow on to light a fire,
you would no doubt wonder
what other miscuts go up
trembling in the smoke.

BUILDING OUR BED OUT OF
OLD WINE CASKS

There are no burrs
or chatter marks.
Every surface is smooth
as the inside of your mouth.

I've concealed my mistakes with inlays,
ribbons of heart-red cypress,
steamed out dents, quelled roughness
with coat after coat of oil
until the pores were filled.

It's cold and turning colder.
The gavelling wood stove can't keep up.
Let's make things so warm
even the wood will be forced
to release its rosewood butterflies.

Don't think you can hurt me by crying.
You have already drunk far too deeply
of somebody else's good wine.

CRACK SHOT

I'm ripping window trim when the old man
who's helping me build my house starts talking
about the time the end of his thumb
struck the glass like a big bee
and landed at his feet in a pile of sawdust.

Before I know it he's speeding
along the edge of a Mobius strip
that twists from his emergency room bill
to the danger of a New World Order,

and muttering to the wall, *we're quiet,*
law-abiding citizens, but don't push us.
Then wheeling to face me, his blue eye
and the brown one screwing
into my missing pocket button,

he raises his voice until he's roaring
the way the wind off the mountain roars
through the trees before it blows them down.
We're a hundred million and we have guns.

Suddenly he stops, and sighting down
the warped piece of pine he holds in one hand,
his nail gun swinging in the other,
turns back to work his wall.

With each crack shot aimed
dead center between the grain,
he drives nail after nail
deep into the offending board.

MY FATHER-IN-LAW'S SHOP

Three rows of hammers:
ball peens, carpenter's claws,
spoonbills for raising silver bowls,
a dozen dead-blow wooden mallets,
racks of riffler and needle files,
pliers, an alphabet of calipers
and scribes, jam jars of brass screws,
drawer after drawer of cutting bits,
and the lathe, on which he turned
fly fishing reels to cast for salmon
in the Gaspe, bone-fish in the flats
of Boca Pila, trout in miles
of Pennsylvania streams—
on this he also turned
a strainer for our kitchen sink.
Mostly, he tied flies
out of condor quills, starling
and ibis hackles, peacock herl.

Like most things, my project today
would be simpler if I knew
exactly what to do:
but I can not decipher
the diagram with its fine print,
and I do not understand how,
using the equipment that's here,
I will ever be able to mill
out of such rough stock
his true smile.

POISON IVY

—for my mother, at eighty-four

I walk slowly
in front of her through the woods
scanning the underbrush.

Suddenly she points to a quavering
leaf. Won't move. Fear that might easily
be mistaken for rapture. I pick the leaf,
press it to my cheek, kiss it—*wild bean*—
coax her close enough to see. I say, *trust me.*

Above us a jay shrieks
take it, take it, take it,

the leaf held at arm's length
the way I remember her
holding the green snake she clubbed
to death in my sandbox.
The leaf's still shaking between us,
no sound in the trees.

THE BAT

Even when cousin Alice dives
under the coffee table clutching
her half-finished needlepoint pillow
of Rudolph and twelve headless reindeer,
David, her PhD shoe store manager husband,
is all for bashing its brains out
with grandma's new Society For The Blind broom
until his daughter starts screaming
she'll never forgive him.
Uncle Jack suggests a net,
but someone points out that bats
can detect obstacles thinner than a human
hair, at which point the twins shriek
as each claps last summer's Make-A-Plate
over her head. A shirttail relative from Queens
suggests maybe it's a vampire.
By the time I decide he's not full of shit,
just joking, he's pulled out a can of Mace
and is waving it threateningly.
The neighbor from next door
who stopped over to return a bundt pan says
he heard that once bats establish their odor,
the only way to get rid of them
is to burn the house down.
He hastily excuses himself.
Millie too, something
about rabies in bat urine,
grabs her bawling baby to find a motel.
Soon, a rush for the door,
and in no time I'm standing alone with the bat
thinking I should have thought of this earlier,
start towards the window.
Suddenly, I realize I can't
let it go. I'll never let it go.

ON YELLOW

I broke my neighbor's nose for calling me
yellow like Martha Nellen the afternoon
she showed me how to make butter
by rubbing a dandelion hard
against the white skin of her inner arm.
Or yellow like the Chinese emperor
who punished anyone else for wearing it,
such was his vast appetite
for what he couldn't bear
to look at directly next to his skin.

Today, yellow is the bee I brush off my neck
as I swerve around a school bus
into approaching traffic,
and our new daughter wriggling in the glass
terrarium at Children's Hospital,
tiny patches protecting her eyes
from the strong light
burning the yellow out of her blood.

Yellow is also the horse I watch
canter across a field of trembling mustard
while the heart of my heart sings
as if it knows the body
must requite the soul, death
grappling us lest we fail to be amazed,
lest love not terrify us—
because otherwise we lose too much.

Be not
afraid
not yellow

GRANDFATHER LOSES HIS MIND

In the mildewed Baltimore row house
I serve him brandy in a gold-rimmed goblet
from the liquor chest commissioned
by a Maryland town for George Washington
who disappointed the people by dying
before it could be presented.

I bring him his genealogical chart,
and as he drags me through a daze
of kings to Charlemagne, I dig
into an ivory Chinese patience ball,
aligning worlds within worlds,
their deep holes and tiny stars.

After supper, he asks me to read
aloud to him from his book, *Water*,
about how the earth is not quite
as smooth as a billiard ball, but far
smoother than an orange.
We play chess. I deliberately lose

my queen. He moans, *oh god, my mind,*
starts for the stairs. Halfway up
he stops, one foot planted on each tread,
and slaps his palm to his forehead
as if by that one blow he might
somehow dislodge whatever it is.

THE LETTER
—May 2, 1839

—then Grandfather kneels down beside the tall
claw-footed Chippendale secretary, puts his ear
against it, taps and palpates, jiggles
the drawers, presses this and that until
suddenly from a secret compartment
he pulls out a letter from Zachary Taylor,
head of The Great Army Of The South,
to my great-great grandfather,
there are too many whites interested
to suffer the Indians to emigrate or make peace.
All hopes of a pacific arrangement must be abandoned.
An occasional murder of a family is of no concern.

THE WHOLE HOUSE

The storm pulls nail after nail
shrieking out of the timbers
until soon the whole house is shaking
and the roof shudders like horses.
Now the shingles are ripped up
and flung flapping into the sea,
the tie beams drawn like long bows,
the windows sucked inward
on a street named after a tree,
in a town named for a lieutenant,
in a country named after the wrong explorer.

GNOME HOME BLUEPRINT
DRAWN BY MY SON

A wiggly *closeline* hangs next
to a little trapezoidal *malebox*.
A path of Cheerios wanders
through a forest of asterisks to the lake,
smaller than the house and with three
smiling fish that inflate it,
and a boat sailing over them into a tree.

There are no doorways. Or windows.
No indication of scale.
And what is that black square doing
in the middle of the bedroom,
and those straggly lines
connecting it to the happy face
in the upper corner
that I had assumed was the sun?

The house bulges with dozens
of square, rectangle, oval tables
scattered everywhichway with little
regard for how traffic might circulate.
Tables poke tables, overlap tables,
too many tables coexisting
in different planes like archeological strata,
or a family living in the same house.

all different
all tables

SUGAR DADDY

He shows up on our doorstep wagging flowers,
and a gift-wrapped package. After supper,
he asks my daughter, *What do you think
is in this box? Horses?* She whispers, *No!
Elves? Bert and Ernie? No!*
Suddenly she grabs the box from the table,
and yelling *candy, candy, candy,*
presses it to one ear as if
she can actually hear the candies singing,
because all at once she starts whirling
around the kitchen singing, and then
he's singing, even the storm's singing
the gladness of caramels, vanilla cremes,
maraschino cherries, until she crashes
at his feet in a heap of giggles.

He helps her up. She hops onto his lap,
sits stock-still while he cuts
the ribbon with a silver penknife,
running the blade underneath the lid,
lifting it off. When she hesitates,
immobilized by choice, he reaches in
without looking, seizes a chocolate
truffle, nibbles at it, lays it aside.
Soon they're both nipping piece after piece
until each finds one with a raspberry center,
until a pinkish stain outlines their front teeth:
his gold one, hers loose and missing.

FATHERS OF DAUGHTERS

Fathers of daughters live quietly
in second story rooms with bars on the windows.
At night they listen to sirens practicing scales,

then on out-of-town business trips buy
a million dollars of accident insurance
and stuffed animals the size of fire trucks.

They pick up after themselves
dreams already small in the distance
that they confuse with love,

so that hardly a day goes by when you
cannot hear them grumbling with instructions
like a storm sent from the North.

Even at this time of year they are digging.
Their shovels and pickaxes speak
sharply to the still frozen ground.

Whenever one disappears from view,
only spadefuls of red earth can be seen
flicking from the deep hole like a snake's tongue.

After the sun has gone down, their daughters
drift softly out of the shadows,
covering the earth with snow.

AT BREAKFAST

4 father poems in a row

when my sixteen year old daughter asks
who was the first girl I ever slept with,
I feel wronged . . . and suddenly I'm back
shaking the bars of the Worcester county jail
begging the guard to smell my breath,
to let me make just one phone call
to Evelyn Belding who's climbing
into the back seat of a Pontiac
with a total stranger.

Do I explain how eight policemen
perjured themselves to convict me
of a three dollar misdemeanor,
all because I had taken their picture
roughing up demonstrators,
or about running into Evelyn
last week in the Gardner Museum
under the missing Rembrandt?

She said she was sorry
which at first I misunderstood
because I tend to complicate love
with danger. *Please be careful,*
I find myself saying as the phone rings
and my daughter is dashing
across the kitchen.
Please.

wow

A LONG WAY AWAY

Down the hill my neighbor is raking leaves
into three piles: oak, birch, threadleaf maple.
But the wind rags them mercilessly.
And there's no end to the skirmishes,
the dispersal.

She will be moving soon,
taking with her the clothesline on which
a solitary vireo used to perch
and my hopes for another thousand mornings
filled with her *t'ai-chi*.

How shall I face dawn without her
floating above the stone terrace
in her nightgown as *Cloud Arms*,
White Crane Flaps Its Wings, — names
sadly comprehensible.

MORNING WITH PINE POLLEN

How clear the water is, and the voices
drifting here from a half-mile away,
but not this morninglit air
glittering with pine pollen.

I'm almost surprised you pass
through it on your walk to buy a newspaper
without so much as a twitch—because,
though people are constantly turning

corners, stepping through doorways,
I find it difficult to watch you
vanish through a wall of sunlight,
then hear you singing as you climb the hill.

Why aren't you hurt, if not upon impact,
then the next instant, light splitting
your body, detaching half of you
from me—before you disappear

the way that hummingbird did
on its trip to the red sugar water,
leaving only an interrupted wing beat
smoking on our bedroom window?

But you look happy, smiling
even as you glance back
and wave at me
through the glittering that stabs skyward.

WRITING IN WATER

Here lies one whose name was writ in water
—Keats' epitaph for himself

It is not like writing in blood:
no vein to open, oath to break.

Just look how it shudders
when I touch my pen to it,
its infatuation with circles,
their escape to the shore
smuggling my text out.

And the illustrations full
of landlessness: fluvial
blues, a rippling
banner of imperial Chinese yellow,

those clouds that float face down
searching for a bottom,
someplace to plant their feet.

Two

TO THE NEXT READER OF THE BOOK
I TAKE TO BED WITH ME

[handwritten annotation: Sexual to the book or reader?]

Many nights before falling asleep
crushed under the weight of mistakes,
I lay in bed with this book,
my fingers drifting over its pages,
their high cheekbones, up
and down its shadowed cleft.

I too once sat in front of the fire
wondering, a little nervous even
about where it might fall open—
to a love scene, perhaps,
or some shocking revelation about sparrows
that would change my life.

Now, I hold it loosely in both hands as I might
a sparrow, imagining you as you are just now,
young maybe, as eager as I am to save
anything except myself, and so close
I can almost feel the brush
of your fingertips, your wanting eyes.

Even when I turn over the book
in my lap to stretch its binding,
or when I fold the corner of a page
I want you to read, and even,
even when I break its spine,
I am thinking of you.

AS CLOSE AS THEY'LL EVER GET

That man in the cherry picker bucket, yes,
him up there in the storm-ravaged tree
cursing the junction box, the pliers,
his cold clumsy fingers,

can he see the woman jogging below him
in iridescent blue tights and ear-plug radio,
her fine strong shape, the easy way
she weaves among the stalled honking?

Wouldn't he wake up each morning
glad for the softest parts of her?
Would she heat his lunch
pail with a steaming thermos,

mend the tear in his orange jumpsuit?   *jail again*
He's been working since midnight
through a buzzing hive of wires
without anything to eat except

a small bag of peanuts.
In half-an-hour, he'll pay
for the pleasure of a cup of coffee,
make that three creams please.

She'll run in place at the light, stretch
her hamstrings on the front steps,
drop her key into the candy dish,
punch the button for messages.

He will deposit his leftover change
in the container marked *Tips*,
his crushed cup in the barrel,
head home to sleep. Only

she won't have a message,
and he'll lie awake in the not-dark-
enough room staring at the misaligned
seam of the wallpaper.

/ great image

wall paper — covers up
a hint there is
something beneath

THE MAN WHO CANNOT STOP CRYING

cries as piously for the souls
of flies trapped between the screens
as he does for whole civilizations.
He cries for small literary magazines,

and for the angels in medieval paintings
grieving for their feet, how
badly they want to dance. He cries
just thinking of flowers in a north window.

And always for the rain forest, the Right
Whales, all three hundred of them, the birth
of too many underweight babies,
the whole state of Christ's earth.

At night, listening to the slow grandfather
clock struggle, he cries for the castaway
bobbing in the waves while the ship sails on,
and for William Cowper at the Judgment Day.

He cries because the bright little girl
and boy stumbling under the glass dome
of their snowy paperweight
will never get home.

But mostly he cries for the *i*'s left
forever dotless in love letters, condemned
to a lover's pointillistic limbo.
And he will not be consoled.

Sometimes he forgets to open his window
so the storm inside can get out.
Mostly the wind just growls in his closet,
clawing the cuffs of his shirts,

but some nights flings hailstones
the size of mothballs at the moths,
or sends squads of miniature dust devils
darting about scattering things.

                  .   .   .

Another night, squall clouds sob for hours
before rain, great hammering sheets
that sweep through the house drench the bed
with memory, a steady downpour of regret.

Then thunder blows out the lights,
and starts firing wildly. Hit,
he'll spend his days tracing that stroke
as it burns upward and out

until the morning he wakes up
frozen in his bedclothes, sorrow
perching artfully on a fingernail,
sunlight hard at work cutting his throat.

BULL MARKET

His barber lathers him with hot
tips on high-tech pink sheet stocks
while the coat check girl pumps him
for inside information. At lunch
he overhears his waiter brag
about the killing he just made.
Even the janitor leaning
on his push broom pauses
every few minutes to eye the tape.

He observes how in the blue
slightly foxed sky a falcon rides
the thermals: circling, tilting,
spinning an invisible thread by which
it slowly lowers the sun onto the waves
of buildings, setting it atop the Old
Customs House where it lies spitted,
exposed to his gaze,
could he but bear to look.

FRANKENSTEIN'S MONSTER

Like any birth, there were discoveries to make,
and small steps toward enlightenment which,
once taken, cut off hope of love, though not love's ache.
Not that he knew either in the crackling current,
or in the first sweet caress of black smoke,
though it did intoxicate him, make him twitch.
Only this: when his father looked at him, he cursed.
Later, he would observe how the girl too shrank
from him, her hands small and nervous like mice.
Could he but have smiled then, told a joke.
Now, finally, he slept, tucked under a blanket
of snow, dreaming of her face. When he awoke,
the sky had cleared. The snow had stopped falling.
Wasn't that his name, his name they were calling?

terrific

out of place

DAPHNE

My legs shook. Hot breath scorched the back
of my neck, mine clawed at my throat
until a blow from his shadow knocked
the wind out of me, and I panicked,

allowing the gods to seize me: every bone,
vein, hair, my voice. And still they demand
I show my thanks each day by trembling
before them so the birds at dawn

to make amends for their long silence
will sing more sweetly. Yet what song
can sooth my rootclutch ache choked with stones,
or unburden me of this crown.

What good are my pleas when the old
gods are afraid to change anything
lest they betray their weakness while
the new ones contend it is none of their business.

Apollo complains of having been denied
his conquest, though I know better.
Like me, he was relieved to avoid the struggle.
He only enjoyed the chase.

OLD LOVERS

ha

Best never to revisit them unless
years afterward, you're still tormented,
or it's late, and you are willing to say *yes*

if one asks you to unzip her dress
in the dimly lighted room you've rented.
Best never to revisit them unless

galloping stallions don't distress
you, or you've forgotten how she once said,
I'm late. And you are willing to say *yes*

to an invitation with no return address
on purple stationery hotly scented.
Best never to revisit them unless

you can bear the heartlessness:
ravaging hands, teeth, a scorched bed.
It's late. Are you willing to say *yes,*

cheap

yes, yes to a devouring caress
despite the wreckage last time you consented?
Best never to revisit them unless
it's late, and you are willing to say *yes.*

IN RAIN

We stood in pouring rain
under a leafless tree
arguing.

You made fun of me,
and I said something I regret,
then stared at my feet
thinking my new shoes would shrink.

A policeman's whistle
broke up a ring of pigeons.
Or were they doves?

I got hungry.

A pushcart pretzel vendor
squeezed sobs of mustard,
licked his finger clean.
Streetlights blinked, and blinked.

OUT OF THE STORM

she stomped in
all accusation no greeting
jabbing
at cushions tilting
the pictures
ripping the glittery air
while the taxi panted
in the driveway
she strode into the bedroom to grab
the ashtray from the bedside table
only there wasn't an ashtray there anymore
she emptied all the drawers
scattering change handkerchiefs
a box of chocolates
when I tried to explain
she stabbed the cigarette
into her palm twisted
flicked it into her mouth
swallowed smiled
lights flickered
the night cracked
I almost expected flames
so when she shook open her fur coat
I could scarcely believe
the beautiful girl who emerged
or make any excuse despite
the terrible risk
I knew I was taking

BREAD

perhaps I am doomed to retrace my steps
under the illusion that I am exploring,
doomed to try and learn what I should
simply recognize, learning a mere fraction
of what I have forgotten.
—Andre Breton

Why do I stay up late at night studying
when entire continents of knowledge
sink unnoticed beneath the waves
into a cold eternal night
where salvage operations are at best
difficult, maybe dangerous?

Inevitable
worthless.

Yet, start me off and I can recite
the prayer for the whole state of Christ's church.
I even remember the number
you wrote on the back of your hand
as we stood above the river watching
the ducks primp the dark water.
I remember the indecipherable
scribble the fish made
when you tossed them crumbs,
and the drafts of beerhall music
shaking the leaves.

When I return to this town of bridges,
I'll cross all seven of them,
ring you up on the off-chance
you're still living
in the same house.

old lovers

Perhaps we can meet for coffee
in some out-of-the-way place
where the waiters don't ask
every five minutes if everything is ok
and the bread is hot.

66 ·

A LONG HOT SENTENCE FOR YOU

Summer's eighth straight rainless week
begins with a tribunal
of storm clouds convening over Boston
ends with yet another ancient rhododendron dead
its thigh-thick trunk split
leaves rolled into thin cigars
each tipped with a glowing nit of ash
as the drought having had its fill
of roses lilacs honeysuckle
hunkers down to serious business
gorging on the rocky carcass of the reservoir
while planning an assault on the big oaks
with still no relief in sight
and not just from this suffocating heat
in which I lie sleepless
a thousand miles from you
but from your searing voice tonight
which opened an ozone hole
through which the past burns.

one sentence

METEORITES

Most burn up trying
to get noticed, or else
throw themselves into some ocean
to cool off,
pockmark the Antarctic —
except for the one
that crashed my party.

Of course the guests went crazy
as they do over anything
from out of this world,
but what a relief it wasn't
that plague of angels
who dug up the garden last spring,
or aliens who leave nothing behind.
And just think, the Smithsonian is coming.

And here is the stone
sleeping in my palm.
And here the ruined tablecloth,
the shattered glass, and up there
above the broken chandelier,
the hole punched through the white ceiling —
that blue sky
fully armed and dangerous.

BLUE

Blue bottle flies orbit me like sighs.
My eyes drowse across a bowl
of shadow, flower, water.

I move slowly
like the snow in a glass paperweight
tumbling through glitter.

There is no currency, no ledger.
In the middle of the night
in a Providence phone booth
I call friends collect.

OHM'S LAW

Over the crackling phone line, he spits
not next week, maybe never
when lightning strikes the mountain
and the sky begins to speak in tongues.

She tries to pick her way back
to him through the static,
the first declamatory raindrops.

Upstairs, her husband closes the windows,
unplugs the television. Sunlight
on the kitchen wall flickers out.
Now her children start crying.

They're much too young to understand why
she turns her back to them,
slumps over the counter hammering
the dead receiver against the wall.

It's suppertime, and they're tired
of waiting for the power to come back on,
which seems to be taking forever.

IN TIME

Fifteen minutes from now,
      when the first fat
raindrops sear the green awning,
the woman I am watching cross against the light
will climb three flights of stairs, knock twice.
Her boss will think she is at the doctor.
Her husband may never know
she is rowing furiously
away from him toward another disaster.

Twenty minutes later,
      just as she's beginning
to moan so loudly her lover worries
she might make too much noise,
her husband, exhausted from all night swatting
an infuriated mob of grace notes will strike
a minor chord on a 1936 Steinway, and cry,
he who has played a thousand pianos,
but never found exactly the right one.

In five hours,
      she will step into the lavender
and civet of the boutique on 4th Street
where she'll be checked-out by a computer
in Cincinnati, and authorized to buy
the splashy red purse
on the arm of the store window mannequin.
The next time she comes in,
the tattooed salesgirl will know her by number.

Tomorrow,
      in the restaurant she will turn
her coat inside out and hang it
carefully on a remote hanger,
attaching herself to its lining with a long thread
that stretches into the forbidden
room at the end of her childhood.
The waiter will keep her glass filled.
Her husband will play Chopin, her favorite.

At eight seventeen,
      the streetlight will flicker,
rain, and more rain, a shimmy of thunder.
The couple at the next table will continue
dispensing their glances through an eyedropper.
When they leave, each with a mint toothpick,
she will still be plowing the pleats of her starched napkin
waiting to penetrate the bones of her salad,
its tender, incomprehensible heart.

In forty days,
      she will have sunk
up to her neck in scented letters stamped Personal,
pale pink ones with their hands out, postcards
hollering Sale, while her boss who's never been able
to scrape the dogshit off the sole of his left shoe
will be shackled and lowered
into the Water Torture Cell
by a troupe of ecstatics bundled in bearer bonds.

Three months later,
          she'll lick
her last Elvis stamp, paste it
upside down on the credit card company
envelope. Her boss will slip out of
his name, sell his terms and conditions,
his collection of Captain Crunch whistles,
and move to Jerusalem in order to spend
the rest of his life getting closer.

A year from now,
          it will be raining
when the woman passes her old lover,
neither of them acknowledging
the other under the green awning.
She will be on her way to the doctor   *for real*
to receive more unfathomable news,
to be stripped and searched, burned
with the cold fire, infected with death.

But five years from now,
          she will look younger
and prettier, while I who now watch over each of them,
want and need all of them — their faltering
arrangements, inane empires of desire —
I who dress them, wait on them, care
like lover and father and lone son
will not be here to remember or tell them
how close they came to not being missed.

MONTHLY

sometimes weekly for thirty years,
through a blur of three failed marriages,
several lunatic affairs, and her dalliances,
so many of them from Florence to San Paulo
that only the most incendiary stand out—
the others merely convenient or cruel—
somehow they managed to stay in touch.
Mostly she wrote on the same dust-blue
letterhead with an old Florida address
lined out, stories about being shadowed
by former State Department colleagues
whose harassment cost her one job after another,
jealous girlfriends who vandalized her car,
old lovers out to get her, and her bit parts
in B movies because the director
liked the way she acted in bed, and once
every few years a plea to make up a shortfall
in the rent—small loans she'd repay with bookmarks,
key chains, packets of Japanese green tea
whose leaves this morning floated in his cup
long after he had pushed them down,
down to where he knew only too well
they would settle in their own sweet time.

GIVE

Tonight as I watch the blue
dragonfly teasing her shaved pubis,
and the gold nipple ring she tugs,
those pearls slithering between her legs,
I wonder, is she turned on, or thinking
how much she wants a cigarette.

Of course, she makes me feel glad,
proud even when she pushes
my folded bill under her ruffled pink
garter along with a dozen others,
and gazing down at me through
the glowing bars of her cage smiles.

Because I am everything to her—
the rent, groceries, a car
payment—she will ride me,
eat me, shatter my wall
of windows, armor of mirrors.

She will dance for me,
lick her finger, shudder
when I hook her eyes. She will even
get down on her hands and knees
and arching her back take my hard-
earned money in her mouth.

DAMAGED GOODS

The room stinks of smoke and Lysol,
the bad breath of the river,
the river's wet banks.

As for the man, when he leans close
to whisper, his eyes gleam
like instruments in alcohol.

And when he touches her,
she doesn't make a sound,
just bites her lip bloody,
and climbs out of a body
that squirms like a stuck bug.

She studies a crookedly hung
photograph of three young women,
their eyes full of a country
she doesn't recognize,
their bodies like piñatas
stuffed with gifts,
their pain not visible until
she touches the frame,
straightens it.
That's the least she can do.

Afterward, she tries
to close their eyelids
as she would those of dolls,
but they refuse to be blinded.

Not that I understand.
All I know is she never
lets me kiss her breasts,
and can't pass by a crooked picture
without stopping to straighten it.

YOUR CALLER

Imagine him cracking
his knuckles fat as cue balls,
a collection of smoke rings assembling.

He closes his eyes
hoping this time you might
mute the television, lean back
in your chair, and listen.

Not that you will understand
the trouble he is having tonight.
He would much rather—if
only he could—hang up.

Because he is very tired;
and tomorrow, he knows, won't
be any easier.

MINE

Mine is the door to the locked
room at the bottom of the stairs,
the kiss hissing from the lips
of the mannequin.

Mine is the heavy sack
into which you are sewn with a cat,
a chicken, a snake.
Mine is the bridge and the river,

and the fish full of maggots,
the lump in your breast,
that brainsick breathing
at the other end of the line.

Mine is the chain letter with the bevy
of pretty stamps that drags you
along the altiplano of money
from La Paz all the way to Reno,

then threatens you with car trouble.
And mine is the driver behind
the smoky glass of the limousine
who runs you over without stopping,

the one who's sent the letter bomb
to your post office box,
set the bounty on your heart,
the one you are rushing to meet.

ACCIDENT

—struck a glancing blow, hurtled
beyond the grimy flame of a tar-lamp,
the blood-marked granite curbstone,
beyond eighty-two dollars and a packet
of air-mail stamps, beyond his limit
on a credit card he can never repay,
beyond the roses blooming
on his denim jacket, this gash in my left
front fender, and the yellow line smeared
with dead frogs. It is not the same
as picking up the hummingbird that drops
into the window box and holding on
to its life while its eyes close.
If only there were
some alternative
to this world.

NIGHT MATH

At which wing beat did the green neck break,
beak crack, head snap back, eye contract?
So unexpectedly and with such impact
it shook the daylight out of the lake.
And how many heartbeats did it take
to run those humming wings at the exact
frequency of a blur? From that subtract
the number of times each night you wake
aching to reach the other side of the bed,
ravaged in wet sheets smudged with dreams,
a hot dark voice trickling through your head.
Now add back the blood earth needs, draws, teems
with. No! The answer cannot be calculated
that way. Yet it's simple. Count your screams.

DIFFERENCE

We are Siamese twins. Each morning
he grabs the sports section,
I the front page. The ice cream
he eats by the quart bloats us,
but so does my bean soup.
He would be happy listening to talk
shows all day. I love Keats.
He can't understand why
I turn down the thermostat at night.
His smoking drives me crazy.
And his table manners!

Both of us look forward to the mail
though I get all of it.
And when we turn our heads to follow
a pretty woman down the street,
he stares at her tits, I her ass.
Differences like that.

TWO HEARTS

Travel to the farthest star,
and farther, then turning,
home in on the heart
where it broods in code.

And the man with two hearts,
what does he have to say
about love? Dare he risk
twice the shock, or run
the same risk twice?

Tomorrow's his wedding
anniversary. Send him roses, long-stemmed
red ones. Two big bouquets.
No, on second thought,
send them here.

BLANCA AND MIRANDA

All year they sit in the back of my class whispering,
best friends exchanging folded notes across the aisle.
At lunchtime, I watch them on the stone steps
combing one another's long black hair.
But now, as they pass in their homework,
I see that each has burned the name DAVE
into the back of her hand.

And I know what that will mean some hot
spring afternoon when they fight in the hallway
or outside on the basketball court:
the danger in stepping between them,
that shrapnel of teeth and Day-Glo nails.
It will take all my strength
just to pull them apart, to hold onto them,
one clutched in each arm, as they rage
like creation and the universe just afterward,
as they flail about moaning,
shudder into limpness.

And when I release them, *Now Blanca,*
you too, Miranda,
they will go slowly, almost dreamily,
late for their next class, and the next.

FROM MY WINDOW

I watch you walk around the block
this raw crow-dark day,
its bitter declamatory gusts.

I should offer you my scarf, my warm mittens.
But I am shy, and sane.
Most likely you'd ignore me
or misinterpret my intent.

I love how you chatter with the squirrels,
skip Ritz crackers across the icy front lawn,
wag your pinkie at a parked Mercedes Benz,
blow a parting kiss
to the big stub-tailed tabby cat.

I hope you'll look up at me.
I'm wearing my yellow hat
as I tease the dictionary to fall
open in my lap to sad longing—

sloe, sloe-eyed, sloe-gin—
which, if I drank,
would be what I'd want now: the tart
deep-blue fruit of the blackthorn,
and dark, soft eyes.

But perhaps you're scared, as I am
of the two dive-bombing sparrow hawks
stuck to the glass above my head.
Perhaps you're waiting for instructions
that it's safe to land.

HELP
—for Wendy Mnookin

I am the man in the yellow hat
auditioning for your poem:
the opening line,
in which I do something despairingly sweet
and desperate like drinking
antifreeze for breakfast,

or a small speaking part,
wholly emotional.
Because I just love
italics, *a deep field*
leaning like blown grass
that eyes sweep across.

I hope you are at the window
watching me scoop up the shit
from my dog, Ars Poetica,
who bears such a striking resemblance to me,
and practice my *t'ai-chi*
in the middle of the wet boulevard

as another morning with its hundred
endangered species of gladness
struggles to stay alive.
Do you wonder why
I am wearing a yellow hat?
It is not because I am bald,

afraid of catching cold,
or even because I yearn
to be in your poem.
I know that you need me
as you sit at your desk
threatened by helplessness, doodling,

beating a path
through ambition to the other side.
Watch carefully
as I take off my hat,
hold its broad brim between my thumb
and two fingers the way you hold a pencil,

then fling it above the unstartled
ducks addling the reservoir
into the fading needlepoint of stars.
Now work, work quickly.
Brush from my shoulder this feather
of sunlight that is crushing me.

MIND

The instant I stuck the thumbtack
into Jimmy Goering's thumb,
I knew. He didn't flinch.
And his eyes clasped the flame
like those of a tortured saint.

Yet, I was stunned when he obeyed,
stood in front of the window on one leg
and pumping his elbows
crowed at the top of his lungs
cock-a-doodle-do-do-do,

when he dropped down on all fours,
barked, rolled over.
And when I said *play dead,*
such stillness lay on the floor
I scrambled for a pulse,
ordered him to get up,
then turned him into a stool,
threw a rug over it, sat down.

Don't expect me to say I'm sorry
because at nine he stopped stuttering,
the manic blinking disappeared.
Eight, Miss Neal gives him a red lollipop
when she moves him
into the red reading group.
Seven, he wins a prize
for the best drawing of a tree.
Six, as the Big Bad Wolf
he gobbles up Bonnie Chadwick
in front of her parents.
At five, when I snap my fingers,
he's smiling.

HEAVY WATER

I help granddaddy make his bath,
bring him singing kettles of well water.
He adds blue bath oil,
a dash of iodine, a tablespoon
of crystal salts that hiss,
dribbles in more hot,
a splash of cold,
then mixes everything with his old
summer-camp canoe paddle, flicks
a few drops on the inside of one wrist,
swirls a fever thermometer through the water
in slow figure-eights,
tilts it to the light.

I steady him on the step
as he slips into the big clawed tub,
hold a mirror so he can shave,
shampoo his freckled sun-baked head,
sponge the boil on his neck, pumice
the calloused nub of each elbow
while he soaks among pillows of steam
talking to me of Achilles and watching
as I kneel on the tile-floor
struggling with the puzzle
he has given me to do: four squares
of match sticks to trick into three.

What if I give up? Should I strike
the matches one by one,
dip them into the dirty water?
Because he has told me it is possible,
and though I know better, I want;
yes, I want to believe
I might ignite it.

KING BEAR

With one swipe
I can crack the skull of a moose
or knock down a pine.
Whoever encounters me suddenly lowers his voice,
backs slowly away.

Those who say I cannot climb have never seen me
swaying in the upper branches
honey coated, dripping with bees.

Whenever you enter my territory,
chant, sing, clap, bang your canteen,
pray that you don't see me.
But should you, wave your arms,
make yourself big.

AMONG POETS
—for Barbara Helfgott Hyett

Everyone arrives late, so we begin
with dessert. My friend swears
that all of us are wired
for language, that poetry
is just a matter of hard work, like gardening.
But I object.
From the crest of the couch Walt Whitman
shouts, *Now dancing takes talent.*
You've got to have legs.
Marianne Moore turns up the music,
kicks back the rug,
Sylvia Plath her shoes,
then grabs a doorknob, yells,
look girls, what we missed.
Williams and Stevens stop arguing. Frost
and Pound, even Emily
comes down from upstairs in her nightgown
and dance shoes, shakes out her long hair.
Yeats joins in. Soon everyone
is dancing with doorknobs.
Except for Keats who climbs up on a big urn
and starts singing: *of deities or mortals, or of both.*

TO A NIGHTINGALE

Fled is that music
—Keats

Here is my ruined vein, a lock
of dark hair, the troubled mirror.

Am I so changed you don't
recognize me? Or is it too much

to ask in the short time left
that you refuse the razor
of silence that craves me.

Please. Just once more. Look,
taste, smell, listen. Touch me
gently. You're disarming a storm.

REQUIEM SHARK
—for Rena

This morning as I gulp five gleaming white
capsules of shark cartilage
to make me strong again, I want
another look at the terrible
eye with its nictitating membrane,
those extravagant fins,
the ampullae of Lorenzini freckling its snout,
all of that huge body on the rippled sand
in turtle grass
with an entourage of neon-blue barjacks,
and a remora wriggling in
and out of its gill-slits.
I even want to touch it again,
and this time not just with my fingertips,
but my palm, loveline and lifeline,
my wrist, the underside of my forearm.
I want to press my cheek against its chaste
astonishing skin smooth as a headstone,
want the touch that feels like a blow,
the summoning touch, the touch
of reckoning, the consummating touch, as well as
the stinging sand blown touch of regret,
the stranger's touch on the train,
the reproachful touch,
even the last touch of a human
who has lain down with a shark,
the touch I have spent my life so ignorant of,
your touch as you unbutton my shirt,
the searing, unbearable touch.

Typeset in Electra, a typeface designed
by W. A. Dwiggins.
Book design by Paul Hoffmann
Printed at The Stinehour Press
in the autumn of 2004.